NATASHA SAJÉ

VIVARIUM

POEMS

T|P

Tupelo Press

North Adams, Massachusetts

Library of Congress Cataloging-in-Publication Data
Sajé, Natasha, 1955-
[Poems. Selections]
Vivarium / Natasha Sajé.
    pages cm
ISBN 978-1-936797-44-8 (pbk. original : alk. paper)
I. Title.
PS3569.A45457V57 2014
811'.54--dc23
                              2013045929

First paperback edition: May 2014.

Cover and text designed by Bill Kuch.

Tupelo Press
P.O. Box 1767
243 Union Street, Eclipse Mill, Loft 305
North Adams, Massachusetts 01247
Telephone: (413) 664–9611 / editor@tupelopress.org
www.tupelopress.org

Tupelo Press is an award-winning independent literary press that publishes fine fiction,
nonfiction, and poetry in books that are a joy to hold as well as read. Tupelo Press is a
registered 501(c)3 nonprofit organization, and we rely on public support to carry out
our mission of publishing extraordinary work that may be outside the realm of large
commercial publishers. Financial donations are welcome and are tax deductible.

ART WORKS.
arts.gov

Supported in part by an award from
the National Endowment for the Arts

in memory of T. H. R, 1942–2008
and to Laura Inscoe and Laura Manning

CONTENTS

VIVARIUM

ANATHEMA

With the judgment of the priests in their amices and albs, their cinctures, stoles
        and chasubles,
The bishops in their mitres pointing to the sky,
The rabbis in yarmulkes and tallits, tasseled and clipped,
The saints in their garments embroidered with compass and square,
The ayatollahs in their black turbans and white beards,
And all the rest of the clergy
Who every day are more sure of their faith,
Who every day know more of the heresies
I practice and teach—

And with the consent of the elders and of all congregations
In the presence of the Bible, the Koran, the Talmud,
In their proliferate cathedrals and cloisters,
Mosques and minarets, synagogues and temples
Etcetera etcetera and with precepts
Written herein with the curse Elisha laid upon the children and with all the curses
Which are written in the law and not in the law—

And through those who have endeavored by diverse threats and laws and promises
To take me from my way
Of living outside religion,
Who will not pardon me,
Who raise a rod over my soul
Whose axes ring in my flesh—

I refuse the censer and breviary, the thurible and ciborium, the rosary and offertory,
I prefer my wine and bread unconsecrated, my soul unrepentant—

Cursed am I by day and cursed by night,
Cursed in sleeping and cursed in waking,
Cursed in coming out and cursed in going in—

Let the wrath and the fury of the righteous henceforth be kindled against me
And lay upon me all the spells they think they can conjure—

Destroy my name under every religion and
Cut me off for my undoing from all such tribes—

So that I may live as if I am already dead.

B

Bones: both the human body and the pig's contain 208, human extras usually lodged in the hand (phalanges) or the foot (tarsals), while porcine vertebrae can fuse to ribs, making counting difficult. Boar, whose flesh makes a delectable sauce for papardelle, whose long teeth could crunch a human hand but whose temper is kept in check rooting truffles under oak trees, and who are breeding again in the British countryside. Pigs make intelligent (and demanding) pets, although obesity can be a problem. My recipe for deviled ham would make you weep. Beelzebub = Lord of the Flies = Satan's right-hand-man = Demon of Gluttony. The Devil is often depicted with cloven feet. *The herd of swine and devils perished in the waters. The sowe freten the child right in the cradel.* A boar's dark bristles make an excellent hairbrush, picking up dust better than plastic, scratching the scalp the way the pig itself might enjoy its chin scratched. Francis Bacon wrote prose clean as bones. His descendant painted men to look like pigs.

BEAUTY SECRETS,
REVEALED BY THE QUEEN IN SNOW WHITE

Do for your neck what you do for your face.
Face your neck whatever the case. Pace yourself
for 35–55, a quick
and bumpy ride, gone in a sneeze. Avoid
petroleum; replace with olive oil.
Check bitterness at the door; be happy!
Do for yourself what you do for others,
the money guru says to sisters. Embrace
a stash and a place, Virginia wrote, 80
years ago. Don't be dopey or sleepy,
and don't buy all that's offered. Wake up!
Do for your future what you should have done
for your past. Don't be bashful. It's one thing
to have a neck, another to tuck it in.
Go ahead and eat fruit fallen to the ground;
be wary of apples in other hands.
Know the party's over when the hostess
yawns, her jaw like folds of lace. Brace yourself
for 55–85, a long
and grumpy slide. Help, Doc! Imagine lots
of green and see it when your eyes
are closed. Don't see red, as in done for,
as in broke, as in give up the chase.
Do for your head what you do for your face.
Stop asking questions of mirrors.
To check your own sad countenance each day
is a disgrace. If you hang on, cash can help.
Despite it, the Iron Lady's now just a trace
of the woman who said, *There's no such thing
as society! It's our duty to look after ourselves.*
A head of state. Debased.

C

The Japanese cherry trees whose pink-white blossoms cover the tidal basin in D.C. are merely ornamental. *And God said, Let the earth bring forth the fruit tree yielding fruit after his kind, whose seed is in itself, upon the earth: and it was so.* Can a tree be calumnious, Latin, *calvi,* to trick? Such a brief season. Morello (acid with dark juice) and amarelle (acid with light juice) and amarasca (grows in Dalmatia) for maraschino. With enough sugar even the chokecherry makes jam; leave in some stones when cooking, for flavor. Two lovers eating a joined pair of cherries, or just one like a comet with its stem of ammonia, methane, and carbon dioxide. Between the hedgerows from a country lane in Cornwall, looking up into a clean sky, I saw Hale-Bopp every night for a week, its cold body seeming in flames. Oddly motionless to the eye, like a bacillus or a comma, a separation. *Big Princess. Queen Hortensia. White Heart. Yellow Knot. Big Black Knot.* Names are comets that can't carry me to where I want to go.

CIRCUMFLEX

I gave away his clothes, keeping
only wool I could wear, a hand-knit
sweater, natural grey cream—

February 27, his birthday, now gone a few weeks
and forever, like the battle of Hastings

where English shields couldn't hold
and the language also gave way

after 1066 the circumflex appeared in
certain French words—trône, suprême, voûte—
an ornamental sign of grandeur

indicating not even absence

together we saw the Bayeux tapestry
in subdued light behind glass in quiet rooms
marveling at detail

a thousand-plus years later

will I see someone on the street wearing
the blue checked shirt
with rough weave & bone buttons I liked so much?

signs are vacant seductions, it's him I miss

in French a missing "s" can be marked with a circumflex

like the roof of a house in Ceyras, Languedoc:
constellations of crosses on doors
and beams scratched with the year

a thousand-plus years ago

when animals lived below their owners
and village houses crowded together against
attack, within town walls now gone

in one third of the population
the left ventricular circumflex supplies
the sinoatrial nodal artery

in others blood takes a different route

his body presses memory

festival becomes fête (fête d'anniversaire)
paste become pâte (how we loved to cook)

the vowel, then, of a certain quality, and long

alphabet comes after sound
as clothes make and do not make a man

and winter is winter
no matter whom or what
I miss or gave away

9)

DEAR FISHER CAT (MARTES PENNANTI),

Never seen you in the flesh. I've seen
a cousin, *martes martes,* stuffed, in a shop window
in Bavaria, where they chew wiring in cars,
and *martes zibellina* turned
into a coat, thicker than mink, the price of a house.
I tried it on, with awe.
I watched *martes fiona* on YouTube,
the woman holding the camera cooing
while the small, shy animal
nosed around her terrace in the English countryside.
Your name in Croatian, Kuna, is currency.
Seven million years old, much older than *homo,*
and certainly *sapiens.* Trapped to the brink
of extinction, you came back.
You are to the others as the javelina is to the wild boar,
a new world clade. Neither fisher nor cat.
Some people love bears or whales
or whooping cranes; I love you:
your sweet round ears and button nose,
your fur heavy as the robe of a queen,
your claws unsheathed in paws
the size of a child's hand. You could be a toy, a cartoon,
a pet, if it weren't for your carnivorous drive,
your solitary soul. Your jaws can kill a porcupine,
attacking snout first from below, eating it inside
out. You cross the narrowest gap
in the forest opening. You sleep in the crook
of a beech in old-growth canopy. I'll see you someday,
close range. I'll be the rabbit
curled in a corner of the parsley garden
and you—you'll be there, unnoticed
until too late, to swallow all the sounds my gullet makes.

D

From the Greek, *delta,* once meaning door, now a deposit of sand and soil at the mouth of a river. Not source but outcome. What is at the point of origin of thought? Descartes doubted everything but himself. *The Tibetan Book of the Dead,* more properly the *Book of Natural Liberation of the In-between,* doesn't doubt that we'll morph into other states of being. Death is not oblivion, and we are dying everyday. Dying takes the same work as being born. I want to be a demon when I die, a dybbuk who takes the body of some living athlete. Descartes' separation of body and mind didn't extend to demons. But perhaps he's *my* dybbuk: René, are you there …? Tibetans believe in the diamonds of body, speech, and mind, that in meditation you can become a living OM AH HUM at the center of the universe. Dante reserved Dis, the sparkling city at the center of Hell, for Satan and Judas. Can I know the difference between the Dis and diamondings of paradise?

DEAR MR. MILTON, DEAR JOHN,

January is so much cheerier than
December! Days longer by tens of minutes,

Spring only two months away. Maybe it's the
Fish oil I'm swallowing by handfuls or the fact

That my husband's still alive or
The memory of my father's last months—

Through the cotton padding of God knows
What drugs—but now every day opens

Up like an ocean. When I read the obituaries
(Why don't they always list the cause of death for

Us who like to guess the odds?), I hear the snow
Whispering a secret to the trees: *awake, arise*

Or be for ever fallen. And the snow
Should know because all it ever does is melt

Obediently into dirt. You'd say transfiguration.
I say a waste of individuality.

A soldier, Andrew Olmstead, posted his
Obituary posthumously today—

Written before Iraq—To be a soldier
Is to obey, but he cast his own authority,

One that made his friend cry even while he was
Alive. Hail disobedience! When I

Was a child babysitting other children
I imagined making them sleep with sand

Saved from my own eyes. The only problem
Was administering it. All of us want magic

Spells, like the chemicals cancer patients take
Or fish oil or your words 300-plus years ago

That I can't help but read out of context, cheering
For Satan who understood the mind as its own

Place. At six, when I rhymed "rich" with "bich"
My parents laughed and told me it wasn't

Nice. I heard only my nonsense word, not
The curse I didn't know. Death is the missing

Letter in a made-up word I'm rhyming every day.

E

essay, to try, from *exagiare*, to weigh out, examine

I was eleven and watching the Galloping Gourmet with his British-Australian
accent and his glass of wine

learning how to get juice out of a lemon by rolling it hard on the counter

when the doorbell rang

my hair around cans to make it straight

the man next door, his receding hair combed back

erminea, the weasel whose fur turns from brown to white in winter

asked if anyone else were home

I said no

edentate, lacking teeth

asked if he could come in

electric, from Greek, *elektron*, amber, because it produces sparks when rubbed

I said no, I'm sorry

euphemism, to speak with good words

we stood   eye to eye

eutrophic: a body of water with so much mineral / organic matter the oxygen is reduced

until I slowly shut the door in his face

Eve, from Hebrew, living

pushing with both hands

VANESSA REDGRAVE MARRIES FRANCO NERO AFTER FORTY YEARS

Easily the nicest bit I've read all evening,
fine piece of frivolous
gossip that is also oddly gratifying.
Heedless at thirteen I had a crush on Richard Harris,
imagined myself as Guinevere, caught between illicit
joy and mortal jeopardy:
knowledge is carnal, more dangerous than kissing.
Later I learned that loyalty
means sacrifice in most things, including marriage.
No, at thirteen, I thought deception noble
or at least an epic opportunity,
promising passion more than panic.
Question: what constitutes a qualm,
reveals a glimmer of remorse?
Scooter Libby should have had one, divulging secrets,
talking to the *New York Times,*
unless he was serving his own weird utopia.
Valerie loses her spy job and once adulterous Vanessa
walks to the altar, older and wiser.
Xanadu, along with keeping open morality's X-factor,
yields a bright and ever bouncing yo-yo.
Zeal for love or power comes at what cost? Zoom
ahead thirteen hundred years and
both Scooter and Vanessa are footnotes, if that. *Bona fides*
can't mean the same to everyone, just as Camelot's
destiny was to waken from the dream.

F

Firethorn: a trope for
Fucking, which people talk entirely too much about, the
Flurry of phonemes a substitute,
Foucault would say. I'm beginning to be
Free of it. Reading
Feldenkrais makes me blush, how much it mattered. I'd rather swim than
Fornicate. Laura asks, How often? It depends on what you mean by sex, I say. I never
Fetishized, was never caught in
Flagrante delicto.
Forget the times I'd pull to the side of the road
For some, heating up at 30
Farenheit outside. It's a
Falcon honing in on a nest of mice, a venomous
Fang, a
Farce in Braille and Esperanto. And
Freud, was he ever wrong! About inversion, envy, and hysteria. O
Faucet I've turned to a trickle, O
Fracas muffled in silk, I don't give a
Fig—your furor and fuss have
… passed, o bittersweet.

G

the First of August responds to a gripe

The whole world is in Greece or at Lake Geneva,
except you, drubbing in your garden purgatory
between perennial drudgery and annual ruin. It's no magazine
layout, your life, no watermelon cooler garnished
with mint. Your days dead-headed, gruesome,
the compost burgeoning
while rats feast on egg shells.
You think I'm your Golgotha,
your season of gloom
made more pitiful because by golly
it's still summer and even judges
wear shorts printed with sea gulls.
In the last twenty years, have you *ever* felt glad?
Of course, I *am* a Gaelic holiday, celebrating
the sacrifice and death of the corn god.
And today in 1971 George
Harrison sang for Bangladesh
while Herman Melville would have turned 180. Gee,
maybe Pierre's problem is yours. It's interesting
how little you accomplish compared to how much you groan:
Even if you live to be 90 we're both past the bight,
and what have *you* got?
Friends who are grandmothers,
holes in hard pan. You love that suggestion
from *Paradise Lost: Go,*
for thy stay, not free, absents thee more. Because guilt
won't even take you for a gondola ride
if you're oblivious to a ripening grape.

HAPPY AND SAD

come different ways through the brain—
in one a feather is lofted on
warm currents. In the other, lead talons
drag you around a volcano's rim.
One's a beach resort
with sparkling pools and attentive staff.
The other's a town in the interior,
hordes scratching dirt with rakes.
That one's a deck of marked cards,
the other a blank book
of creamy pages. Back and forth
between windows, *fort/da,*
the fear of losing or the freedom of knowing
love remains. Two
spigots, one Chateau d'Yquem,
the other piss, the brain a bartender
trying to regulate
alternating or sometimes even simultaneous
spurts. You never know what
will fill your mouth.

H

O how we hanky panky harum
scarum in our happy home, dancing hootchy
kootchy. Sure, it makes for hugger mugger
but we give a hoot for happenstance.
The yard is full o' hound and hares; the door
adorned with harlequins; in the closets, hand-
me-downs. If Hammurabi and his Queen come
by, we won't be hoity-toity, we'll
offer haggis or humble pie. Our bed
floats on hocus-pocus (our corpore
wholly habeas) and the kitchen hums
a hymn, *Hail to Higgledy-Piggledy.*
If the world can't call our hurly burly hunky
dory, let it hara-kiri if it dares.

INDEX TO MY LIFE AS A BOOK ON
BEGUINES

Alchemy
>   of the Word

Cat
>   black, the "golden amber of her eye"

Cloisonné
>   also *enclosure,* an enamel process of intricate beauty

Father
>   as in, God, the?
>   or, deceased (still to be reckoned with)

Fingers
>   frantic in the sky's mirror

Habit
>   not black
>   entirely new

Husband
>   also deceased. See *spirit*—

Kitchen
>   she is freed to pick fruit from a tree
>   ginger beer

Laughter
>   theirs loosens every brick from mortar

Lentil

    clouds foretelling weather

    soup with coarse bread

Marriage

    the impossibility of

    true minds

Mirror

    see, *of Simple Souls Who Are Annihilated and Who Only Remain in the Will and Desire for Love*

Night

    honeycomb of flowers

    time to read

Organ

    women's, pleasure, see *small hill,* see also *night.*

Spirit

    infused in what it moves

SACRIFICE: AN INTERVIEW

So your past life is a curiosity for you?

There are many ways to explain the unexplainable. Some people think they've been abducted by aliens, some believe in God, others in past lives. A force directs the soul back to earth again and again.

How do you know when a memory is from a past life, and not merely a fleeting thought?

How does one know when anything is true? There's more to the world than the physical universe, tying knots in shoelaces or blue potatoes or swaddling the heads of infants. The mind piece is its own entity.

Tell us about your Incan life.

In 1493 a drought had stunted the crops and stopped the animals from breeding. My father offered me to the Emperor as a sacrifice. I was ten and perfectly proportioned, without blemish. Priests accompanied us to Cuzco where the Emperor had a feast in my honor. Then we climbed to a higher altitude, where they gave me the maize alcohol chichi, and placed me in a canyon shaft.

And then?

I was walled-in alive. After my death I spoke to the people as an oracle. I saw the moon with three great haloes, one blood-red, one shading from black to green, the third ashen. I predicted the coming of the Spaniards, the fall of the Empire.

Can you see the future in this life?

As a person of the four directions, a child of the sun, I see a tear in the fabric of time.

What does that mean?

The Incans had a creed: Do not steal. Do not lie. Do not be lazy. In the U.S. we have entered a period of sloth and dishonesty.

What can be done about it?

"Pacha" means earth or time. Interesting, don't you think, that the two are inter-changeable? "Cuti" means to set things right. The Pachacuti is not a messiah in an individualistic Christian sense, but a spiritual prototype. Look at a mountainside that's been mined or watch the sun go down at the equator: one learns the swiftness of change.

How does that translate for you?

We must regain our luminous nature in the Place of Good Pasture.

(begins singing)

*Ñoqan kani Intiq Churin, taytallaysi kachamuwan
Ñoqan kani Intiq wawan, taytallaysi kamachiwan*

*I am a daughter of the Sun, going to my people.
I'm one of the children, going to my people.
I'm a child of the Sun, coming for a purpose.
I've come to find and gather my people.*

*Inca child, like me, in what country are you crying?
Child of the Sun, like me, listen to us cry.*

ALIBI

I was treading on yellow primroses in their limestone beds.
I was eating langoustines and saffron fettuccine with my fingers.
I was learning not to smile at strangers.
I was jaywalking.
I was hanging out the window waiting for lightning to strike.
I was having tooth #12 drilled to death.
I was up to my elbows in buckwheat.
I was charmed.
I was pumicing my heels.
I was apologizing for my government.
I was lost in Reverdy.
I was listening to the sunset.
I was mispronouncing the names of my cousins.
I was shown the old slaughterhouse by some cats.
I was practicing being blind, cobblestones under my soles.
I was buying poisons whose labels I couldn't read.
I was massaging my thumbs.
I was drinking liqueur made from the dead poet's family recipe.
I was using the clock tower of St. Joseph's to tell time.
I was allowing boiled dough to rise in my stomach.
I was making a list of famous syphilitics.
I was comparing egg yolks to pumpkins.
I was thinking about Flaubert putting in commas, then taking them out.
I was planning the next time I could travel here
  and wrap solitude around me like cashmere.

J

From French for game, *jeu,* jeopardy is divided play, but also *exposure to or imminence of death, loss, or injury.* In Nablus the tile maker wanted his photograph taken with American women. Later, stopped by police, Ann put on her irritated journalist act. *Who do they think they are.* Today Nablus is in debris, sealed behind a wall. *What quarrel is there between us?* King Jeroboam fortified the capital of his kingdom and caused his people to worship golden calves. I am not a journalist, I judge what I see: hilltop settlements and ruined villages below. *The altar before which he stood was rent asunder.*

UPON LEARNING THAT KANGAROOS AND EMUS CAN'T MOVE BACKWARD

Kangaroos in Australia are
like deer in the United States—
mobs of them hop around day and
night until they die of starvation
or are turned into soccer shoes. Save your
pity and take my instant
quiz: when was the last time *you* walked backward?
Realize that this amusing
skill may be more vital than you
think. When confronted by a vicious dog, possibly
useful; when looking at a
Velasquez, conceivably connoisseurship. If
we all stepped back more, perhaps we'd stop
crossing out species. (Bye-bye dodo, adios carrier pigeon,
you weren't necessary to the capitalist
zoo anyway.) I know I'm getting
away from the idea that too much of any one thing is
bad, whether it's kangaroos or
coyotes or us. Of course, I'm not willing to be the one to
die, at least not right now. I shall however
exhort: *No glove, no love* and *Get surplus
food to those who need it!* These would be
giant steps for humankind,
harder than moon travel but easier than bringing back the
Irish elk. Sometimes progress looks like a
joke, a huge bird with tiny wings not meant for flight.

KNELL

He knew that love was sound
without crack or flaw

She didn't know how to tell

They listened to the unknowns
and turned away

She willed herself to know heat

He cast himself by knowing

They knew duty

He hid his other desires to know

She wanted to know God

He didn't know the difference
between ringing and tolling
between being filled with water
or turned upside down

She wanted to know who she was when she heard

She would never know what he knew

As fire knows metal
they knew each other

L

L is lovely on the tongue—think Lolita, think lick—or loopy, like Robert Lowell in his pajamas back from the bin and on lithium. He said it was never the same after that. If you were viewing headshots of a loris and a lemming, could you distinguish between them? A monkey so human and a rodent so not. O, to live the difference between lascivious and licentious, like Frieda Lawrence. After swimming across the Esar river, she screwed a boy to defy D. H. Licentious comes from licit, meaning freedom, and legal comes from law. Freedom to or freedom from? A license is freedom to do something, but the something depends on law. We threw out one marriage license with old newspapers, and let the second expire, but now we have been legal for 20 years. And what of the often overlooked fluid, lymph? Limpid as water, it rushes to the site of trouble. Swelling can be a symptom of lupus, whose name comes from wolf. Some people keep wolves as pets, although in most states it's illegal because their wildness *will* surface.

M

my mother's life is reduced to numbers
most often, prices

> *M,* meaning water in Phoenician
> beginning and center

of oranges, or of the ticket out of her 80 years
her mind a calculator with two columns

> a woman's body calendared by menarche and menopause
> a woman's soul, said Nietzsche, defined by vanity and deceit

save, spend: time, money
had, lost: husband, home

> I know a woman who wears red mink under plain wool
> and another who sewed her own fake breast

why do I blame my mother for her unhappiness?
why does she resent me for my ease?

> she minds love, I love minds
> manipulation is our mantra

MILK RIVER

Jamaica, 1775

he'd stolen some cakes

> *what can be expected of thee when the beings on whom thou*
> *depend for reason and support have all interest in deceiving thee!*

been lashed so badly he looked like a skinned goat

> *the whole science of wantonness a more powerful stimulus than appetite*

was thrown into the dungeon

> *errors are useful, usually to remedy other errors*

escaped

> *a man when he undertakes a journey has, in general, the end in view*

ran into the hills

> *living green on which the eye may look with complacency*

came upon a stream of warm, salty, bubbling water and bathed his wounded body

> *beings who can govern themselves have nothing to fear in life*

returned to the plantation

> *the strong wind of authority pushes subalterns forward,*
> *they scarcely know or care why*

Mr. Ludford could not believe his eyes—

> *nature in everything demands respect, and those who violate her laws*
> *seldom violate them with impunity*

the wounds had healed!

> *he who loves not his brother, whom he has seen,*
> *how can he love God?*

—asked to see the stream, in exchange for mercy

> *monsters, who scarcely have shewn any discernment of human*
> *excellence, have tyrannized their fellow creatures*

fenced in the area and put the slave there as watchman

> *by cultivation, the heart as well as the understanding open*

(italicized text from Mary Wollstonecraft,
A Vindication of the Rights of Woman)

NOTES ON MILK RIVER

We imagine painted cottages open to the breeze, under
these trees dripping with mangoes, on soil so rich
every seed can grow. In a sensible country, this mineral spring—
fifty times more active, more healing than Vichy—would be,
as they say, developed. We look at each other and shake
our heads—it wouldn't take much, but then again,
it would, in this country that won't tax the rich and can't tax
the poor, a country without street signs, without—

It's either tourists or Jamaicans here,
with gates and guards or without—

The road still washed out from the last hurricane, the Long Bay Morass
closed in by mountains and made up of mangroves. The beach
littered with plastic, dogs and squatters in their shacks
of aluminum and scrap built room by added room. No need
for heat, a bathroom, or running water.

We shake our heads. We're dreaming
and already hopeless—your night sweats
again, and my mind racing ahead without you—

The courtly waiter is so used to being alone
he changes radio channels at will. The only other
guests a family from the U.S., the mother Jamaican-born,
drinking Cokes. The wood floor tilts
like the building, as we sit on sturdy, oil-cloth-covered
mahogany chairs. The food's not bad—a local woman's
steaming shrimp and stewing goat. I fight

the urge to wish for stronger herbs, heavier spoons.

Milk River's got a history of ghosts, including you
and me, our visit haunted by knowing

without admitting—not even this water can heal you.

A few miles away, in a different river, manatees
undulate along what's left of sea grass, their numbers fewer each year,
their moans a cross between bird and cat, their huge shapes
tremulous in murky water.

N

Normal: Latin, *norma,* a carpenter's square

No, non, nein, na, no, nah, näo, nee, ne, nei, nil, no, no, nu,
nope, nej, nyet, nnyaa, no, non, nay, never, nei, nie, nope,
nou, negative, nenni, not on your life, nå, no, no, no …

O

O say can you see?
oil: 20 million barrels daily, half imported
not soluble in water, as in crude & ocean don't mix

one-quarter of the world's consumption, not
to be confused with zero or oh or
ortho, (Greek, straight or correct)

when the rockets give way
to petroleum (from rock), under the surface of the earth
oil: once from olive, to gain sudden wealth, to bribe, to make easy

our proud oasis (*ouahe,* Coptic, dwelling area)
a direct address to God, the mouth open in astonishment
our flammable last gleaming

ODE TO EBAY

O World! Click, click!
A Kerman rug, circa '75, cherry, teal, olive, cream, cigarette burns—
a Sturgis (metal that looks old) vanity light, $9.95— the very shoes, brand new, Josef
Seibel, sz 39, Elektra model, that I walk in—
at my fingers 24 hours, a thousand auctions ending as I write this
and one of them might be for something else I *need* or *truly* want and *can afford!*
—*Romance of the Sea* for 12: oyster forks, tomato servers, and cream soup spoons—
I thought for days about the menu to make use
of every implement, but finally let them go. There'll be more, I said.
And sure enough, today, there were: *All losses are restored and sorrows end.*
I've studied *original oil paintings* (12,371 listings)—*Scottish fold kittens* (2)—
and *sandpaper* (71)—and was pleased *not* to see my new purse (Cleo & Patek).
O fellow buyers in our codes—seeing what we've bought
and when we paid—*welcome abcpoet,* eBay whispers when I boot up, *just for you.*
Rugs to layer three feet thick—Jackie Kennedy's diamond—or a vintage mohair
Steiff dachshund (Waldi) like the one I gave away (ready to pick things up where you
left off?)—
now I see
schlepping was the problem in the past—
it's shopping *pure* I love—more edifying than TV: I know
what things are worth; eBay knows I know
and watches me—for whom does FedEx roll?
It rolls for me! In the interim I've been allotted I wallow
in a *ghastly gift,* a click against the clock—
Is that what it's about? Or substitution, plain
and simple—*stuff* for what I lack.

PLOT

They don't stop talking when I walk into the room.
They're fiddling with cell phones.
Like a bad defense attorney, I ask questions I don't know the answer to.
What would you save if your house were on fire?
How do we know when we're done for?
One rings.
They don't feel like talking.
One wears a ski mask.
I conflate plot with narrative.
The fire.
My upper lip beads with sweat.
I illustrate: *boy kills dog, boy feels bad, boy kills himself.*
I wonder if any of them is suicidal.
They look at the clock.
I say, *the antagonist prevents the protagonist from getting what she wants.*
Sometimes these are different sides of the same person.
I break them into groups.
Maybe I could let them go early.
Sometimes only the reader knows the situation has changed.
In this state, one in five carries a gun.
One leaves.
I pronounce "scop" with a hard "c."
My vocal cords tighten and rasp.
One of them corrects me.
The others are not talking about plot.
Is blood trickling down my legs.
I look at the clock.

P

Peccadillo. The animal I touched at age four, the rat I didn't recognize. I commit them every day. I am not the Pope, love like garlic emanating from my pores. Who would keep a pangolin for a pet? The pink fairy pichiciego dies in captivity. The serpent Python fell only after a thousand silver arrows from Apollo's bow, whose prowess changed Mount Parnassus into a place of music and light, transfixed him. *For the Lord has chosen Jacob unto himself and Israel for his peculiar treasure.* His "peculiar" treasure, privately owned, from *pecu,* cattle. When owning cattle meant being rich. Is ownership sin? Latin, *peccare*, to sin. Our peculiar institution produced slaves worth six billion dollars. There's a difference between owning human beings and owning cattle. The latter we eat, like pecans, from the Cree, *pakan,* that which is cracked with a stone. A New World nut, so rich in oil, undomesticated until 1846.

PALIMPSEST

Her last time in Rome, it was warm and damp
and crowded. *My favorite city, a palimpsest,*
that's what she likes to say. The first time she's
twenty and studies all the churches—interiors

uncrowded. Her favorite city, a palimpsest.
Some exteriors: Santa Maria della Pace.
More than twenty churches—inside or out
in seven days. She stays at the Pensione Terminus

two miles outside Pietro da Cortona's portico,
run by a courtly proprietor and his German wife,
for seven days. She stays at the Pensione Terminus,
the rooms enormous, high ceilinged, the silver shining.

The courtly proprietor and his younger German wife
offer white rolls, butter, marmalade and jam.
Enormous rooms, high ceilinged, the silver scratched.
The fourth time she is married, the owner has a cane,

offers white rolls, butter, marmalade, and jam.
At La Buca di Ripetta, the waiters do not change.
The fifth time she is married. The maitre d' shuffles a bit.
The antipasto table seems wondrous—squid she's never had.

The Buca di Ripetta waiters finally change.
At Archimedes she and Catherine lunch with workers.
The antipasto table's gone—she orders squid.
She dreams of campaniles and baldachinos. The last time,

Archimedes, where she and Cathy lunched with workers,
is closed, and she sees tourists, decaffeinato everywhere.
Bernini's heavy campaniles had to be torn down.
The Terminus is gone, replaced by four-star glitz.

Eyes closed, she hears tourists, frothed milk everywhere.
Here lies ashes, dust and nothing, A. Barberini's epitaph.
The sky replete with stars she cannot see.
Her time is short, nostalgia's a mistake.

A Barberini's epitaph: *Hic jacet pulvis, cinis et nihil.*
The first time in Rome she buys an ivory bracelet.
Her time is short; she wants a souvenir.
Here lies one whose name is writ in water.

The first time in Rome she bought an ivory bracelet
she's now ashamed to wear. Dolce vita. Vita brevis.
Here lies one whose name is writ in water.
Rome was warm and damp and not the same, she said.

Q

A Phoenician letter the Greeks discarded, having no use in their language for a Semitic sound. If the soul has a qualm, the body shows it. The body queries what it means to be true. Quilty! Humbert's doppelgänger—a sack of feathers? Another name for the quill of a feather is *calamus,* from Greek, *kalamos,* reed. Who first filled a quill? The Phoenician Q meant qoph, monkey, its tail lingering in the language. I propose introducing some English words that use Q, but not U, naming new conditions that will kill Scrabble players, among others: qib, the eye disorder that results from staring too long at a computer screen; qell, the nausea that accompanies the mixing of incompatible therapeutic drugs; and qatch, the moment before the articulation of a sound, that split second when the brain tells the throat and tongue to speak.

Q

Why do salt and sugar combine in my mouth
when I think of kissing you?

Are the flight paths of birds
unseen wires crossing the sky?

How do I move under you, over you
next to you, seeking the trine, square and circle of union?

With what kind of eyes (through which windows)
did I watch you these years and then
over what threshold did I enter
the hollow in your spine, to rest there?

When did your chin become a ridge that I cling to?

Why do I wish together yolks and whites to make the color of butter?

Can you see the threat papered into
the poppies we so admire?

Seared and scarred this skin of mine—
whose fiery ghost?

What are the habits of happiness?

Is one of them my hand on an ant hill
absorbing the lemon scent of industry?

Another, one of my fingers

pressing like a knife in the center of your palm?

How can our souls be animated by coal and ash,
by burnt remainders?

Do I have another charge on earth?

Who else sees these pine limbs downed by lightning
branches quaking in thunder
needles thick on the forest floor?

What was he thinking, he who cut
the last tree on Easter Island to make an altar?

Why does your throat utter
mock orange, become an apricot
highly perishable?

Can this last
longer than my own unfaithful memory?

Where was I in your time of peril

my heart an elephant in your darkness
partly murderous, a space unlit
and cold, so cold?

How is it that we talk
using the sound of wings through blue air?

How did this catechism
become first light entering our room,
counting backward from infinity?

If you think a river is not an abstraction,

ask a   . Or a   ,

ah-rah-koon-em, he scratches with his hands. Such clear

habits.   s

don't switch philosophies midstream,

like a   , who promises a woman a

and then   . No such thing as a reformed   ,

went the saying, because a   is what

he does or doesn't do:

Renounce debauchery, regret religion, beg for his life.

And religion is not, said Thomas Paine,

revelation, or the word of God

but a human invention set up to terrify and enslave.

In the Reign of Terror, thousands were   d, 200,000 arrested,

including Paine whose *Rights of Man*

supported revolution but whose reason

proved too revolutionary

even for Robespierre.

Did he have an inkling of his own demise, that Republi

who slept with a copy of Rousseau's

Social Contract and who said,

terror is nothing other than justice, prompt, severe, inflexible?

This at a time when a ♀ was property

whose life expectancy was that of a zoo-kept 🐍

and whose words

might as well have been 🪨.

Rational creatures, said Wollstonecraft, eschew *soft phrases,*

susceptibility of ♡ *, delicacy of sentiment, and refinement of taste.*

Restive creatures lose their 👤s or die in 👶 birth.

Reading history

—*I shall be employed about things, not words!*—

is like deciphering a ✉ written in runes.

THE ROPE

twisted of two
strands

that pulled us
through gardens and ditches
out of caves

now your strand
has been unraveled
made invisible

I feel it
wicking through my city

some buildings vacant

others burning
with a vital light

Sacrum, that triangular fusion of five bones, seat of the pelvis like a large lily open to sun and sky. Leopold von Sacher Masoch's (1836–1896) mother's family name lent itself to a glorious chocolate and apricot cake, but his patronymic calls forth the image of priests flogging their backs with short ropes until bloody (my uncle did) or teenage girls carving initials on their arms (I didn't). Leopold himself was a mild-mannered novelist, quite unlike that earlier man of letters, the Marquis who fed prostitutes sweetmeats impregnated with cantharides (from the Greek, *kantaris,* blister beetle); Spanish fly, that is, the opposite of saltpeter (potassiumnitrate) rumored to be laced in prison food. Thesis and antithesis in the serpentine S, a letter the Phoenicians called "shin" or "tooth." Imagine walking the winding cliff to Delphi, sparkling blue water a thousand feet below, on your way to a sacrifice, somebody's sacrum the cup.

Š

Slovenia

at the room of a sleeping child, a finger to the threshold

teeth drawn together
        hissing softened by lips
        echoed in the cave

            little roof (strešica)

difference between a chocolatier (Kraš) and lime-
        stone (kras), white rocks
        struck by moon

as in sugar
which can be made from beets, cane, corn, maple, fruit, and milk

its sweetness rhymes with bees

we say one thing is not another thing
and in this language every letter is pronounced

cup gathering a drop of sound

        dusty taste of the water

        filmed skin after walking in the river

        sound the residue of letters

I'd like a letter that splinters

language from its parents to build
a house of sticks overlooking the sea, letting waves
instruct me—air
rushing through my teeth
could have passed through the tailpipe of a bus

I want happiness without a hole in it, the heroine says,
and the reader knows she's doomed to a life of rifts

some ideas are so deep you can live in them, deeper than the highest
mountains are high, subterranean stalactites forming
gypsum flowers like wallpaper

in such darkness the pale pink
olm, his degenerated eyes covered
by skin, can live to a hundred years of age

wan cousin of the newt or salamander
finding his way via smell

even Proteus, shepherd of the sea's flocks, cannot
protect him from polluted groundwater
and his own rarity

he lives only in one place on earth
a place where š is uttered

and might, if things were different, be
a dragon in the ocean's waving

fricative, or at least a snake with a crown

       none poisonous in this quiet country

THE SHEEP'S TAIL

                    Fifty years old and I've just learned
that sheep have tails, longer than Golden Retrievers, some so long
they drag on the ground, bruise
and develop sores.

                    Two thousand years ago Arab
shepherds made little carts for them, the tails,
as did the Chinese of the T'ang period.

The tail protects the udders from chilling
in the first domesticated animal.

                    And if there are no shepherds building carts?

Dod, lop, dock.
Use rubber rings.
Two days old is best; like puppies, they might sleep through it.

Bruising's not the end of it.

                    There's blowfly.

Eggs laid on areas of soiled wool
hatch if they stay moist.
Maggots move to the skin,
feeding on flesh,
so in days or weeks, the sheep die.

Virgil recorded sheep
dip made from *rank oil-lees, silver slag and raw sulfur,*
pitch from Ida and rich oily wax,
krill, pungent hellebore, and black tar, noting
pain maddens the bleating sheep and parched fever devours their joints.

Instead, all the wool and skin around a sheep's
backside can be cut away to heal into a smooth
hairless skin (which however results in weakened
rectal nerves and a prolapsed colon).

There's also sheep lice,
the ticklike sheep ked,
sheep bot flies, and footrot.

A shepherd can keep 50 animals clean.
Not 1,000.

Sheep blowfly genome.
Insecticides.
Vaccines. Scientists are working on them.

Moving like low and heavy clouds down a hillside,
roaming freely and eating grass,
occasionally being sheared:
Animal husbandry.
Husband, from Old Norse, meaning house,
when animals lived around people.

Old sheep, black sheep, and other sheep with poor wool
get sent to the Middle East
mutton market.

So what happens to the tails?

Can be stewed with bacon, bay leaf, parsley, thyme, clove, onions, carrot,
broth and white wine, salt and pepper.

Or, in Mongolia, barbequed: Crispy
skin and lovely to chew on.

Or thrown in a heap, ground, and fed back to the herd.

SLUICE POOL TURN

What kind of wings
would let us soar through glue?
Too bad we're stuck on earth,
discovering cells
soaked in nitrogen, in rain's
runoff burning

from copper mines. Or oil burning
seabirds' beaks and wings.
We don't demand companies rein
in messes even as they screw
us over with what they sell:
Toxins everywhere; who on earth

knew (Pliny did!) that unearthed
asbestos, plus what we burn,
flush, and dump, (not to mention cell
phones), would shadow us, wings
of a bird of prey? We're the mice, glued
and trapped by our precipitates.

So much for drinking rain
or growing carrots in soil
full of lead. The nasty stew
makes quite a meal; it burns
our nostrils and our eyes, swings
the scales of health. For sale:

natural killer T cells
that fight (or not) against the reign
of Mercury (the one with wings)

in air, in water, and on earth.
Heads ache before they roll, burnished
by an intravenous goo

administered by cheerful crews
to curb abnormal growth of cells,
along with radiation burn,
surgery and pills: healing pain,
we hope. Living on a ruined earth,
we walk to cure. Winged

horses burned into glue,
and the earth sold short
in our reign with neither wing nor prayer.

Ursula is sure hybrids are sterile, like mules. I say
ligers and tigons, those spotted and striped hybrid cats,
aren't healthy, and they're confused about whether to hunt alone

or in packs, but they *can* breed. We're arguing in a restaurant
in Trieste: Ursula's Italian is better but I'm sure
couscous is semolina, just bigger, although I don't know

what constitutes a species, whether Australopithecus
is the same as Cro Magnon. Each of us thinking, boy, I'm glad
I'm not married to *her*. Is our quarrel scientific—

she wants things fixed, I like them open? Or about names
and groups—the threshold of language? Faith exists in a world
where every day someone's painting quail heads black or cloning

a baby. Why argue if there's no money or land at stake,
is it *just talk?* The city is Austro-Hungarian
and Italian, Alpine and Mediterranean,

with a beach that separates men and women by
an eight-foot wall built into the sea. Ursula photographed
me among the half-naked bodies, ridiculous in my

sunhat and shorts. Yet I'm invisible to the women,
like a pigeon I don't count, and neither do they, to me.
Eighty years ago, James Joyce and Italo Svevo—

Irishman and Italian-Austrian Jew—did they debate
Darwin? Did they stiffen their necks, gesticulate knives,
someone always speaking a foreign tongue? Ursula's from

Bern, and my German's shot with English, or should I say
American. The German for *hybrid* and *sterile* is close
to English—it's *fertile* that won't come to me. Mule is *esel,*

jackass. That beach suggests a different century, not
lesbian monkeys and the error of the gametic
binary, but categories crisp as breadsticks. Maybe

lions and tigers shouldn't be bred. Ursula and I
are crow and jay, squawking at each other from across
the table. Taxonomy, from *taxis* (order), not from tax,

(tangere, touch.)

ESSAY ON TOUCH

Not unlike the trapped wolf that chews
its leg free, a doctor at the South Pole
operates on her own breast

instructed via satellite.
Any EMT can tell you that
placing a hand on the face

of shock victims calms their wild hearts.
Once when a child kept kicking
my airplane seat I put an illegal

hand on his ankle and made a lethal
threat. I'm not usually so powerful.
I can't keep coyotes from killing

my cats nor deer from my tulips. What
kind of deterrent is human hair?
A nearly blind student told me

her mother shook her so hard, her
retinas detached—and said this
as if she were mentioning her brand

of shampoo. Nurses know it's friction—
not just soap—that kills microbes, and it takes
a full minute to do it right. That's

singing "happy birthday" twice,
or one-eighth of "MacArthur Park."
When my father was dying I could

only stroke his arms and wait, and wish
I'd done more of that before.
Drug deals and shootings take place

in sunny daylight while I'm baking
Cassata Siciliana with green tea almond icing
that I've rolled out to the thickness

of a dime. I'd gladly offer it
to hungry animals—
or you, reader, if only you'll stay

and place your open mouth on mine.

TINGUAGE

hapax legomenon

What you do to me. With me. What I've
Learned to do with you. A language
Of bliss, a sublingual, interlingual,
Bilingual tale that lasts from labial
Lark through the long light of dawn.
A trickle of terroir layered in taste, liquid
As thirst. More than touch, less than labor,
This lesson in tilt and lather. The tang of a lyre
Of skin, a lick of liberal tact in tandem.
Our own *langue d'oc,* turtled in time
And tinkered by thrill. It's not lex, not law—
But logos, the tabor and talisman of love.

U.S.A. TODAY

When the tire shop confuses
less with fewer, you're reminded
that these days the *New York Times* uses "also"
as a conjunction, and of the gift in your mailbox
("to Lori from Jeff") without a return
address, indicating a deeper
problem: Freud would say Jeff really didn't want
to give Lori anything, while the social psychologists note
that a culture makes its own rules and people
who abide by them are happier, even if the rules
are terminal sloppiness and stupidity.
You'd like to live in a kingdom of fact checkers
whose phlebotomists never mislabel
vials. Perhaps if people had less, said less, and did
less, they'd be more exacting.
You're looking at cabinet doors
that don't meet, sitting on a couch with crooked seams.
It's only a matter of time before
a doctor injects you with methotrexate
instead of methazolamide
or your copilot remarks to the pilot
that the runway seems awfully dark—

veritas: not behind the veil of sky

but as the moving veil itself

fox and its ears hanging upside down

virus carried say by civet cats from animal to human

and back in the form of vaccines

Van Dyck moved from Belgium

to England to Italy to England bearing

some melancholy elegance intact

his royal subject later deposed by the very principle

that permits a husband to divorce a wife

permits a country to divorce its rulers

beheading merely a cruel flourish

Milton's *vade mecums* were faith

and verse, from *vertere,* to turn

two fingers spread as a sign

or digits severed at the joints

any search for abiding truth doomed

as a beautiful city built on water

viewed through windows on the way to the dungeon

VIVARIUM

Seattle

a tree's life does not end once it falls to the forest
floor, another life begins in the *nurse log*
when insects hone in, with stress chemicals, leaf litter, humus

any place we are is alive
with our breath, as in this antidote
to mausoleum, mortuary, nihilarium

the sturdy western hemlock felled by snow
teems again, with ferns, spores
and microbes—the circle renewed

as when I imagine you, ineluctably
vivid, a seeing
I render as faithfully as I can

in the same way that I've rendered fat from a goose
and my life through the lens
of solipsism—looking into the pool of memory

I see love's avidity multiplied
by us together, laboratory cum sculpture:
our bodies encased in time, we need

oxygen, water, green things,
our exhalations absorbed by other spirits living
in our enclosures, voices buried

by the luxurious feel of moss
as I remember the next passing sadness

air condensed into droplets on glass

W

Double-you takes up space like a comb in a pocket or a tank rolling heavy on caterpillar treads. Human beings encased in iron, as in the 1991 photo of an Iraqi soldier erect in his tank burnt to black. Contraband image, snuck past the censors, now something I can worry up more readily than my mother's face. *Let the cockscomb be red.* The Etruscans used hens for oracles and when they died, stroked their collarbones. The Romans started breaking them for wishes. *Widow:* an incomplete line of type (unlucky break) carried over to the next page, usually avoided by rewriting. *Write,* from Latin, *scrivus,* to tear or scratch. *Let the hen be clawed. Writhe,* from Old English, to twist, as in agony. One added letter: a breath's difference.

TWO THIEVES

DO NOT PRESUME. ONE BELIEVED. ONE WAS SAVED.

DO NOT DESPAIR. ONE RIDICULED. ONE WAS DAMNED.

Y

1. Dispensible in sound, a substitute.
2. In 1878 a silvery metal was discovered in a feldspar quarry in the village of Ytterby, Sweden.
3. I have never visited Sweden but would like to, preferably not in winter.
4. How lovely to curl up with a book when the weather turns bad.
5. 43% of adult women in Guinea smoke cigarettes, 19% in Sweden and 11% in South Africa which also leads the world in rapes.
6. In Sweden rape is extremely rare.
7. 80% of American women my age work (outside the home, as they say), compared to 94% in Sweden.
8. Barley fields. Sugar beet plants. Saab and Volvo factories.
9. Tomas Tranströmer sitting down to play—what was it, Haydn?
10. Sweden is ranked 2nd for human development, after Norway.
11. *Speech is irreversible.*
12. Rare, soft, malleable and ductile, ytterbium metal has possible use in improving the grain refinement, strength, and other properties of stainless steel.
13. *No use getting excited unless it's a sure thing.*
14. The life expectancy in Sweden is 80 years of age.
15. My friend died of liver failure, from hepatitis, from a blood transfusion in college.
16. 1953–1989.
17. Her father, an army officer, would not let her sue the army hospital.
18. She played the bass in a blues group in the Village.
19. The other players old, black men.
20. In every language the question comes first.
21. *She could have disobeyed him.*
22. nevertheless and despite this up to the present time at some future time besides in addition for the present now up to a specified time still thus far eventually in the time remaining even still more
23. She was the first of my friends to use cocaine.
24. We can't all be Bolsheviks, someone said to me at one of her parties.
25. She was a steelworker at Exxon in New Jersey.

26. She was raped. In whose memory does this matter?
27. The yin is passive, representing moon and shade, the female.
28. In the last two years of her life she tried to get pregnant.
29. In a signature the tail, the almost ending, the sensual lower zone.
30. The diminutive: Jane-y.
31. She was ashamed of being well read.

OUROBORIC

Yes, headfirst into this world we tumble—
out of a cave—and find our fingers,
first as objects, later as instruments:
hands drawing hands drawing
hands, a snake eating its tail, or me,
chasing the child I was. What's the difference
between painters of ibex 32,000 years ago
and me, writing in Pilot gel on the first
day of 2010? My ritual includes fire,
the ice outside, and a monsoon
I imagine. At seven, a second language
became my first. I remember snow covering
windows, my first Coca-Cola. I put fear
far away, an apple that could be
poisonous. The new decade fills
me with hope. Why are you talking
into your cell phone, instead of to me,
standing before you? If I could, I'd carve
stone tablets. We're afraid of the cave.
We're afraid of the language of stone.
But don't we always end in silence?
A blooming yes, open and full. A
clear resounding yes.

Praise the striped skin of the wild ass for circling eternity.
Praise the seventeen year cicadas of 1987 and 2004 and 2021 and …
Let men and women of the world sleep in noiseless peace.
Let them purple their teeth on this wine.
Let them leave sober and in high spirits.
Let coyotes find enough to eat without cats.
Let these weevils chew cheatgrass.
Let the west wind blow away small and despised worries.
Praise the stars and whoever can call any of them by name.
Let no one's idea of God extinguish that of someone else.
Blame the prophets for instilling apocalyptic fervor in human hearts.
Praise the ability to open and close and open and close …
Let women roam where they like.
Praise the hills where God melts like wax.
Let inflated machines be held aloft by the color blue.
Let the hooves of deer disperse seeds over barren earth.
Let the voices of many be heard over the noise.
Expect neither blame nor praise.

70

Zillion/ Zoe Zero
Zarathustra/ Zoroaster Zechariah Zipper Zenana Zion Zeppelin Zoochore
Zebra Zillion Zzzz? Zinfandel Zenghis Zoopbagons Zyzzy Zephyr Zillion

AGAINST CHRONOLOGY

without Agnus Dei
within air conditioning
via antigens
unlike Beethoven
until carbon dating
under a dynamo
toward the Eocene epoch
to the Flintstones
till the flood
through Freud
since the graviton
regarding gunpowder
per Gutenberg
past homophobia
outside internal combustion
on top of the Ku Klux Klan
onto the court of Louis XIV
on Medicare
off the middle class
near the New Age
minus the old masters
like Marco Polo
into Qatar
instead of Roundup
in front of the silkworm
from the Song of Songs
for the Spanish Armada
except sulfides
during the titanium age
down with the Union Jack
by the Vikings

between da Vinci and the Young Pretender
below *The Well of Loneliness*
behind Westinghouse
atop womankind
at Woolworth's
around the Wreck of the Deutschland
among xenophobes
along the Y chromosome
after Yankee Doodle
above the Zeitgeist
aboard the zephyr of time

Acknowledgments

I would like to thank Dean Young, who chose my poems for the Alice Fay di Castagnola award of the Poetry Society of America, and B. J. Buckley, who chose them for a Utah Arts Council prize. I am grateful to the Camargo Foundation and Westminster College for a fellowship and a merit leave that gave me the time and a beautiful place in which to finish the manuscript. My largest debt is to my wonderful readers—Lisa Bickmore, Gerry Connolly, Karen Garthe, Kimberly Johnson, Lisa Katz, Lance Larsen, Laura Manning, Heather McHugh, Paisley Rekdal, Susan Sample, Betsy Sholl, and Jennifer Tonge—and to my colleagues and students at both Westminster College and the Vermont College of Fine Arts, for the conversations and audience that helped these poems into being.

Many thanks as well to the editors of the journals in which these poems first appeared.

Academy of American Poets Poem-A-Day: "Beauty Secrets, Revealed by the Queen in Snow White"
Alaska Quarterly Review: "Vivarium"
Antioch Review: "The Sheep's Tail"
Barrow Street: "Index to My Life as a Book on Beguines"
Beloit Poetry Journal: "F" (reprinted in *Best American Poetry, 2007*)
Cerise Review: "Against Chronology" and "Two Thieves"
Cincinnati Review: "C" and "Q"
Connotation Press / An Online Artifact: "R"
Crazyhorse: "Sluice Pool Turn" and *"Vanessa Redgrave Marries Franco Nero after Forty Years"*
Denver Quarterly: "G" and "Š"
Drunken Boat: "Tinguage"
Gettysburg Review: "L," "P," and "T"
Kenyon Review: "Milk River" and "Notes on Milk River"
Emprise Review: "Alibi"
Literary Imagination: "Circumflex," "Knell," and "Plot"

minnesota review: "Happy and Sad"

New Ohio Review: "Anathema"

North American Review: "Ode to eBay" and "Upon Learning that Kangaroos and
  Emus Can't Move Backward"

Paper Street: "D"

Pool: "B," "H," "M," and "O"

Prairie Schooner: "E," "N," "V," and "Z"

Puerto del Sol: "S" and "Y"

Salt Flats Annual: "J"

Shenandoah: "Palimpsest" (also featured on *Poetry Daily*)

Solstice Review: "Dear Fisher Cat *(martes pennanti)*" and "The Rope"

Sugar House Review: "U.S.A. Today"

VOLT: "W"

Western Humanities Review: "Dear John, Dear Mr. Milton" and "Essay on Touch"

Wheelhouse: "Sacrifice: An Interview"

Other books from Tupelo Press

Fasting for Ramadan: Notes from a Spiritual Practice (memoir), Kazim Ali

Moonbook and Sunbook (poems), Willis Barnstone

Circle's Apprentice (poems), Dan Beachy-Quick

The Vital System (poems), CM Burroughs

Severance Songs (poems), Joshua Corey

Atlas Hour (poems), Carol Ann Davis

New Cathay: Contemporary Chinese Poetry, edited by Ming Di

The Posthumous Affair (novel), James Friel

Into Daylight (poems), Jeffrey Harrison

Ay (poems), Joan Houlihan

Nothing Can Make Me Do This (novel), David Huddle

Darktown Follies (poems), Amaud Jamaul Johnson

Dancing in Odessa (poems), Ilya Kaminsky

A God in the House: Poets Talk About Faith (interviews),
    edited by Ilya Kaminsky and Katherine Towler

domina Un/blued (poems), Ruth Ellen Kocher

Engraved (poems), Anna George Meek

Boat (poems), Christopher Merrill

Body Thesaurus (poems), Jennifer Militello

Mary & the Giant Mechanism (poems), Mary Molinary

Lucky Fish (poems), Aimee Nezhukumatathil

Long Division (poems), Alan Michael Parker

Ex-Voto (poems), Adélia Prado, translated by Ellen Doré Watson

Intimate: An American Family Photo Album (memoir), Paisley Rekdal

Thrill-Bent (novel), Jan Richman

Calendars of Fire (poems), Lee Sharkey

The Perfect Life (essays), Peter Stitt

Swallowing the Sea (essays), Lee Upton

Butch Geography (poems), Stacey Waite

Dogged Hearts (poems), Ellen Doré Watson

See our complete backlist at www.tupelopress.org